T0103989

Of the Moment

An Anthology of Verse

Carolyn Rose Durling

Order this book online at www.trafford.com
or email orders@trafford.com

Most Trafford titles are also available at major online book retailers.

Print information available on the last page.

ISBN: 978-1-4907-6579-2 (sc)
ISBN: 978-1-4907-6580-8 (e)

Trafford rev. 11/05/2015

www.trafford.com
North America & international
toll-free: 1 888 232 4444 (USA & Canada)
fax: 812 355 4082

Contents

To Mum, who still guides me from the other side.

Many thanks go to my family and friends, for their endless support and encouragement. A special thank you to my friends Jayne for her hours of patience and understanding while editing this book, and to Edna who collated, and made sense of my scribble.

"By standing on the shore of imagination – your mind can cross continents."

An Anthology of Verse.......

KNOCK ON WOOD

I selected carefully what I should say
and how to word my poem today,
with my serious head on I decided to unfurl
what's currently going on in the world.

On second thought, would it be best
to leave well alone and not be a pest?
Should I make people laugh in light hearted prose,
or would that get up someone's nose?

Perhaps a tear jerker, to tug on heart strings,
or maybe some lyrics for others to sing.
A spiritual piece to uplift the soul, or
a tip or two on how to reach your goal.

I finally decided to just be myself,
and to do the best that I could
with what's in my head, apart from the wood.
I've nothing to lose, and perhaps something to gain,
so I've reached the conclusion, it's been worth the pain,
and leave it to you to decide if it's all been in vain.

PAST TIMES

I hankered after passing times!
Threw caution to the wind.
Re -kindled flames, where only embers had remained.
Yet! Still somehow expected yesterdays to be the same.

I fired my imagination!
Walked down memory lane in trepidation
lest my thoughts betrayed my pain.

I stealthily gained a foothold
within my hearts domain.
Reluctant to let go of that tiny flickering flame.

Then I gazed into the future, and saw what I would lose,
by living in past memories, I knew I had to choose!

So! One last glance, then the picture dimmed.
I had dampened the flames smoldering within.
I poured oil on troubled waters, and decided not to swim.

At last my values sorted, my turmoil passed the test.
I had exorcised my demons. My ghosts were laid to rest.

I am looking to the future, my heart feels so serene,
and when I look behind me, my past is nowhere to be seen.

GYPSY DAWN

I dance in the gypsy dawn!
And pile the stuff of dreams
on the back of a unicorn.

I run in corn ripened fields!
And sour on winged heels.
I'm Destiny's child!
Beautiful and so surreal.

I catch moonbeams of silver light!
I place them under my pillow at night!
And drift away on a cascade of stars.
Pure delight!

I float on a passing cloud!
Proud, and feeling serene.
An incredible sense of belonging,
shows heaven is all that it seems.

I walk on the stairway of life,
knowing I touch paradise.
My journey now almost done!

I dance to the gypsy fiddler's strum!

IF I ONLY HAD WINGS

Babbling brooks, sequestered nooks, rainbow bright, sheer delight. Happiness overflowing as cascading waterfalls, and memories catch their breath in the wonder of it all.

Kingfisher swooping down to land on a silvery lake, and as a wistful breeze wafts by in a light-hearted mood, just touching my face with a featherlike kiss, I am entranced by Natures beauty such heaven, such bliss.

Glowing and golden warm as can be, I am content, relaxed and so gloriously free. How wonderful my life so full of positive things, you know I really could fly, if I only had wings,

A CANDLE HELD HIGH

A candle lit vigil!
A cry rent the air!
What happened?
Where are you?
Does anyone care?

Sweet charity. I beg you hear my plea.
They didn't die
from illness or disease
but from madness,
the modern man's curse
upon humanity.
As we hold on to faith,
in silence we stand,
paying tribute, and homage,
to the youth of our land.

Still as statues, united,
candles held high
praying for peace,
that no one else dies.

United in grief
divided by war,
can you answer me this?
What's it all for?

SOW THE SEEDS

Beware the wrath of stormy thoughts, and still the mind of angry deeds.
For once the seed of doubt is cast, nothing lasts.
And who can blame the recipient for tasting sweet revenge?
Then again, if one refrains from casting doubt there is nothing to shout about.

So if we take heed of inner calm, and charm instead of harm,
how innocent our thoughts, how pure our acts of charity,
when with clarity we see the goodness of our deeds.
Knowing this time we have sown the seeds of positivity.

I FELT THE RHYTHM OF THE BEAT

I felt the rhythm of the beat, so did my feet!
Around the campfire we sat. Hands in lap
fingers tapping merrily, as swirling round and round
the dancers almost lifted from the ground.

Such was their fervour! Such was their grace
as faces alight with heat and pace
they stamped and clapped, not catching breath
so intent on happiness, of feeling alive.

I sat mesmerised! Watching with sheer delight,
as these special people shared with me
the secrets of their history told through dance.
They swayed as in a trance, free of care.
Of me they were unaware.

I had stumbled upon their Gipsy camp
quite by accident, and been welcomed
as if they knew me well.
I could tell they meant me no harm
felt no alarm, as they took my arm,
and bade me stay.

How colourful, how wonderful it felt
to be part of that place, it made my heart melt.
Such kindness was I shown that day,
as I had temporally lost my way.

Now I feel that I'm on track,
I'm ready to go back, to return
to who I really am, as I ride up
front of a Gypsy caravan.

I thank the lord that I was lost that day,
I'm home and here I intend to stay.
No longer will I feel alone,
or my heart feel heavy as stone,
I'm alive, light, free, as I sway gently
to the beat, and dance with happy feet,
I share the campfire, share their song,
I'm here where I should have been all along.

ALTERED TIMES

Lay bare the soul of mortal time,
enhance images of silver screen
and flicker into life
the stuff that's made of dreams.

Twilight's coming into view,
and endless ticking times
fail to see this through.
As blowing cool, like autumn breeze
they hold fast with bated breath,
and charm the clock of reality,
allowing us to rest.

Changing shades of altered time
remind the night to slow,
as winter turns to spring,
then summer plays its sweetened chord of longings
and autumn makes its show.

Hold fast the memories as tides are turned,
and tuned waves of sleepless imagery
flow once more into mind,
knowing now with certainty,
only fools are blind.

REALITY IS BORN

Fantasy wakes up the soul

and energies stretch and yawn,

mirroring enlightened times

as in their wake reality is born.

SWEET CHARITY

The pain subsides, but never dies.
Life pulsing through veins into a broken heart,
trying to stop the fear that's tearing me apart.

My aching head tells me I'm not dead,
yet I deny the waking hours. Just let me sleep
for in raging torrents of self-pity I steep
 my emotions, boiling in a frenzy of doubt.
Why? How did this come about?

I cannot see sweet charity,
for my eyes are blinded by reality.
I won't see him anymore!
He's gone, my feelings raw.

How can I continue in this vein?
I feel I must go insane.
Unsanitary thoughts fill my head,
tempting, thrusting ideas of self-destruct
into my vision, blank, unseeing, shaking hands.
Oh Lord I'm stuck in limbo land.
Where did we get it wrong?
When did his feelings end,
or had the rot been there all along?

And so I rise! It's another day.
No different from yesterday.
I pray that sanity returns
so I can escape this impending doom,

this torment, this total breakdown,
this hated room.

"Ah! She's awake. Come on Jake,
help me get her in the chair,
we need to wash and brush her hair.
She has visitors today.
The Doctor says we must keep her calm
so she does no harm,
after all we don't need bad press,
here help me with her dress."

 "Just a quick jab, there's a good girl,
look she's calmer now, anyhow,
just spoon in the rice, don't want her messy,
there that's done, don't you look nice?"

I don't understand, what's going on?
When he left he said "I won't be long"
Ten years they tell me I've been here,
but full of drugs I feel no fear.
So why won't they send me home,
I'm quite relaxed, what could go wrong?

The headlines read.

 "Man Found Stabbed In Bed"

The story went!

She calmly gave her statement
as to why this man was dead.
"I couldn't let him leave" she said.
"He was messing with my head,
so I just stuck the knife in deep
and then went back to bed".

The sentence read.

To be detained indefinitely.
She's quite insane, so inside
these walls she must remain
never to be freed again.

The light is dim I cannot see,
sweet charity, please have mercy on me.

IT'S NOT TOO LATE

Light glinting on tempered steel, raised to kill.
Human blood spilled needlessly.
Greed the reason for those slain. Without gain!

Enlightened times? I think not!
What have we learned from past atrocities?

Have we evolved since King Richards knights,
fought in the crusades for religious rights?

Have we turned the tide since Hitler ruled?
No! Think about his cruelty, can't you see!
Today there are many Nazi scum around,
little Hitler's still abound.

How many times have arms been raised?
How many sharpened blades used to kill?
Yet! Still we haven't had our fill.

Greed steals its way along furrowed minds,
I want what's his he wants what's mine.
How long before we turn the tide?
It's up to us as nations to decide.

It's not too late, we have a chance.
Let's not dance to another's tune.
Or! Once again the dark ages loom.

Let's raise our hands in friendship,
we can soothe those furrowed lines.
Shall we walk as one into the light?
In these most harrowing of times.

MIND BODY AND SPIRIT

Shamanic healing, singing bowls,
Angel wings to enfold lost souls.
Buddhist temples quiet and serene,
to wash the mind and body clean.

Enlightened beings shining their light
on all who ask, to uncover the mask,
so they can become one with the Universe,
and step out from the dark,

A cure for all ills, a wealth from above,
a spirit cleansing and healing, it's called pure love.,

Hidden deep, deep within our souls are Shaman,
Buddhist and singing bowls.
Angels herald a brand new dawn,
as awareness and enlightenment are born.

Safe in the knowledge we have all this
we welcome our spirit home
with a kiss from above.
How pure our souls.
How blessed with love.

FORGIVE ME MY SINS

I saw him lying on a park bench!
Wrapped in the Daily News.
Clasped in his hand an empty can,
there were holes in his worn out shoes.

The stench as I passed that park bench
made me want to heave, I couldn't believe
the state he was in, and on the ground
I spied an empty bottle of gin.

Now forgive me for my sin.

I never even bothered to stop
to see if he was ok, I just hurried past
eager to be on my way.

The following day, I passed that bench
a crowd was gathered round,
I asked someone what was going on,
they said a body had been found.

Now forgive me for my sin.

My informant said the guy had been dead
since yesterday afternoon," It's a shame"
he replied as I enquired "that no one had
known he was there, but to be fair, even if they had
would they have really cared?"

Forgive me my sins.
For looking the other way.

Now each day as I pass that bench in the park
I leave a can and a bottle of gin.
It's for the spirit of the man with the hole in his shoes
wrapped in the news taking his boozy snooze.
The guilt that I feel lives with me still,
and I know that I'm paying the bill.

Forgive me my sins.
For I know I never will!

SECRETS YET UNTOLD

Crystal – multi facetted – multi dimensional.
Glowing – sparkling –myriads of colour,
Dominate the prism of light alive with
Hidden contours – hidden meanings.
Fire bursts as stardust exploding the myth of Atlantis.

Secrets as yet untold – as yet untouched,
Yet still they lay fathoms deep, caressed
By languid emotions locked forever in time.

Until that is! An enlightened soul not yet born –
Still to be chosen from the realms of spiritual dreams –
Just waiting, content – happy in the womb of eternal love,
Until they burst forth uniting, one with the other –
Life in all its beauty – Innocent – as yet unsullied
Pure waiting – just waiting for the right time.

A time when all we know and have known,
And all that is still to come, succumbs to an overwhelming
Desire to cease to exist.

Then, and only then, can crystal clear vision be visited
On the enlightened ones.

Time returns this time in perfect order with the universe.
Atlantis has risen – her penance done, and once more, she takes
her place in the universal order of things.
No longer courting danger.
Peace at last in a near perfect world.

THE UNDERWORLD

Welcome to our world the fairy sang.
She fluttered on the April breeze,
Her gossamer wings splayed as a fan.

Iridescent colour filtered through her hair,
She danced in gay abandonment totally without a care.

One by one, until the glade was full,
Fairies, elves, leprechauns all answered to her call.

Come spring is here, join us as we celebrate
This wondrous time of year
And! Suddenly alive with joy,
Not caring as they listened to the breeze,
Birds of every description settled on the trees.

Beneath the undergrowth, no longer bare,
New buds springing upwards, blessed by morning sun.
A whole new life of animals shook themselves awake,
Their sleeping done.

Watching in fascination this magical scene, evolving before my eyes,
The wonder of it happening brought tears, glistening,
And, to my surprise, I cried.
The honour bestowed on me that day
Stays forever in my heart,
And I know the spirit of it all will never go away.

INSANE LANDS

Lay bare the soul of innocuous crime.
Drive home the force of sequestered times.
Play tune upon the cord of discontent.
For in its relevance, the facts laid bare for all to see
will decide upon the course our lives must take
in truth and honesty.

A fetid world! Hearts turned black
by anger, fear and "I want that."
But! That's not right, the lands are theirs.

What gives you the right to make them fight,
to ignite a powder keg of vicious hate,
stop before it's too late!

Let the children sleep safe at night
in their own beds, it must be right
do you not see their fear and fright?

A beacon dazzling bright, shines its light.
on hopelessness, and in the hope of resurrecting
sanity in these insane lands
drapes it's fingers of pure love over ice cold hands.

Hoping to melt ridged cataleptic states,
to waken up those soporific times
a promise made long ago still stands,
one that will see you giving back those lands,
because you see Divine intervention is at hand.

LILAC TIMES

Beyond the corners of reality
just waiting to be found.
Tapered thoughts of lilac times
shape contours of the mind.

Sweet charity smiles so sublime
and lifts the veil of consciousness
on rustic fields of dreams,
as a blush of rose beguiles,
tempting and serene.

Evocative and innocent
nostalgia plays its part,
as with a gentle nudge
so lightly does it brush,
even an enlightened soul
would hardly feel its touch.

As lilac turns to purple hues
dipping into night,
so does the memory of life,
pull down the shutters of the day
until that is, the spirit comes out to play.

FOREVER THERE

Love fans the wings of celestial joy.
Finding ecstasy in cooling breezes,
Waving their fingers of iridescent drapes,
Shadowed only by the depth of their being.
Hallowed expressions smile at longings,
Still on the lips of tomorrow's dawn.

Visions cloaked in mellow thoughts
Try successfully to be recognized
As positive attitudes.

No more uncertainties, of as yet
Undiscovered virtues.

No more the indignity of bared emotions,
New born and naked in their infancy.

A BRAND NEW DAY

Rain splashing against the window pane
like tears falling from my eyes.
Wind tapping gently on the door
silencing my sighs.

Shadows casting purple images,
on walls within my mind,
and darkness strokes my vision
leaving me vulnerable and blind.

Night time voices assail my ears.
Longings cling to fractured thoughts,
emotions misted, insincere, tumble
into pools of doubt.

Caught in tangled webs of memories
not to be allowed the freedom of respect
my heart cries "let me out, what has this
journey been about?"

The rain stops, no more tears.
The calming winds tame my fears.
Noise abates, darkness gone,
purple shadows bringing dawn.

My heart sours unshackled, whole again,
so my journey has not been in vain
just for a while I had lost my way,
and now it's the start of a brand new day.

For as shadows alter
Allowing future promises,
So, awareness bows gracefully
In acceptance of life's new promise,
Smug in the knowledge of unbroken vows.

Sacred, unsullied, forever there,
Forever there.
Forever.

WHAT PRICE LOVE

My tears fell as raindrops upon my cheek.
My sobs came so fast I could not speak
my heart beat so loudly I could not hear
and what was the cause of my distress?

Loneliness! A fear of being on my own
so alone, no one to tell my troubles to,
no one to say," I'm here for you."
no one to say "It's all right I will stay with you
all through the night."

Sadness comes in many forms,
I'm sitting here so forlorn, heart torn,
through countless hours of torment
and strife. Is this to be my life?

Should I perhaps be content?
Be in my element for the year's I've had,
or do I have the right to be sad?
Sitting here in my own "pad."

They tell me just how lucky I am,
three meals a day, my own bed pan.
"Now listen Gran it could be worse,"
says my own appointed nurse,

"After all it's not everyone, who's
lucky enough to have a son that
pays, so you can stay in an old folks home,
you should feel blessed, not distressed."

Night time falls, like my tears,
no one to hear or see my fear,
no one to say "It's ok I'm here to stay."
They close the door and go away
with "You be good now don't make a fuss"
ringing in my ear,

Another tear falls upon my cheek,
and another as I start to weep,
for all the years I gave to my son,
yet he could not even give me one.

What price love my son?

From your ever loving but heartbroken MUM.

HOLD ON SWEET DREAMS!

Inside my dreams float memories of time and lands, long ago.
of people, places, ideologies brought forth on a new days dawn.
From somewhere deep inside my thoughts, names conjured up
remain forever in this sacred place.
Things will never be the same.

Our journeys take us different ways; life's edicts say it is so.
Yet!

Once more on the thread of life, I hang, reluctant to let go.
Our future is uncertain.
Our past has been and gone.
But!

This time!
This space!
This moment
Is as a never-ending song.

Hold on sweet dreams!
Don't wake me yet.
Don't show me reality.
Please let me bask a while in white oblivion

Because!

I know that when I rise my memories will be gone.

INNOCENCE

Return my child to your innocent state
do not let fate destroy your dreams,
or hate sully the mind of wistful times.

As a rose blighted by disease,
wilted unnourished tangled by weed.
Hold your face to the sun
for you're not alone, blossom my beauty
crawl from under that stone.

Take my hand, trust in your faith,
you have done nothing wrong.
It's no disgrace, you have to survive
in a world that's corrupt.

So what! You stole from that man over there
he just passed you by without a care.
That you had no shoes on your feet,
only rags on your back was of no consequence
to him in his personalized Jag.

He dropped his wallet on the floor
as he opened the car door.
I saw you chase after him to give it back,
all you got for your pains was a hard slap,
and told to move or he'd call the cops,
so you ran my child and didn't stop.

Hold your head up high, know you tried,
survival is what is important now,
carry no sin, the sin lies with him.
An innocent child defiled by doing what's right,
sleep easy in your bed tonight,
for the good Lord knows you tried your best,
so slumber in dreams good night and God bless.

A CHILD OF TODAY

Freedom respects ideals, and reasons understand intellectual ideologies.

On the wings of enlightenment goes the fear of injustice and pain.

Setting forth in turbulent waves of sincerity, reasons become logical in their quest for understanding.

Trepidations steals its way along furrowed fields of dreams, as stark reality becomes softened, by tapered thoughts – and longings become possibilities in a never-ending struggle to identify the self.

Now perhaps I know who I am!

I am a child of past longings; I am yesterday's shadows and tomorrow's promises.

But! For now, I am a child of today.

IN GOD'S NAME

The night is still!
I long for peace
in this warring world
it's so surreal, the way I feel.

Why must you kill,
and spill blood,
was not two World Wars enough?

Have you not learned from past mistakes,
the loss, the pain, the dreadful hate?
What will it take, for this to change?
Please don't fight in God's name.

He asks you remember the apple Eve ate.
Stop this carnage, before it's too late.
This was never intended to be your fate.

A beautiful world, free to us all,
clear skies, silence, no bombs to fall,
that's what the Lord had in mind,
when he created these lands,
so why do you foul up his plans?

What would you do if left up to you?
I dread to think, I really can't see, why? Why,
people are put through this misery.
Is it because money's you're God,
hidden under the guise of it's for their own good?

Do you not think we have enough on our plate,
in a world where the natural state
gives us plenty to worry about? Stop!
Before it's too late, concentrate
on the matters in hand, it's not about winning,
because before very long there will be nothing
to fight over, our lands will be gone.

Not destroyed by man's greedy hand,
can you not understand?

Mother Earth has had enough.
She boils and bubbles ready to erupt,
you've signed our fate, she's finally buckled
crippled with hate can you turn this around?
God only knows!
Just pray, it's not too late.

Love conquers all, so you're in with a chance,
the pipers been paid, no need to dance
to others tunes, listen to the message within,
understand you were born free of sin.

Let all return to that wonderful state,
make love, not war, eradicate hate,
I know you can do it, it's now in your hands,
don't foul up again.
Make it as Custer's last stand.

AN EXTRACT FROM MY RANTINGS
ON A MISERABLE EXISTENCE

How can I wreak such havoc on unsuspecting souls?
The flame diminishes, but the spark remains.
Scotland the Brave!

Ne'er tac' a quill to paper in anger, or in misery, for once written
it can never be denied, only if the receiver burns the evidence.
Once gone – so be it.

When aye the soul burns with indignation, a traitor to the cause,
wee bonnie lass, step back from pride and sorrowful indigestion.
It robs the gut! Defiles the cross we aye are sent to bare.

A lighted candle! Tapered! Dulling near its end, shows aye the
real need for yonder dawn filtering through strands of whispered
words not formed, yet!

A thought! A thread! Sown into the fabric of the mind.
Whist awake dull thought, none would know it's there.

Hark! The lilt of yonder pipes.
Fragmented.
Wailing on the wind!
Aye ages gone ta who knows where it enters with the dawn.

Aye! Snare the trap with bated breath.
Anger goes with time.

UNIVERSAL PLAN

A teardrop fell!
Like ice, the cold air crystalizing breath immortalizes time.
As shattered dreams, the droplets freeze.

One, then another, more and more,
Until cascading waterfalls of pure emotion
Smash into a thousand fragments to lie in pools of crackled ice.
Held motionless in frozen dreams
Waiting till the edge of dawn
Brings forth a natural warmth to dry
This liquid proof of sadness.

And yet!
Without these weaknesses
Laying bare our immortality
How could we know our strengths?
What better way to be a man
To know now who I am
A droplet falling into place
In the universal plan.

MY ANGEL

She floated on a cloud wrapped in crystal dreams.
Her hair as fine as silk lay billowing round her face,
I cried!
No disgrace! As wrapped in gossamer wings
my Angel brought to Earth her special gift of love,
my darling child, my precious boy and filled with joy,
I thanked the Lord above.

My Angel smiled in her delight,
she had stayed by my side all through the night,
waiting for the dawn to come,
to hand to me my new born son.

Her tears of joy mingled with mine,
her goodness given to my son
will see me through when times are bad,
you see I've just lost his dad.

My life, my companion, the only one,
never got to see his son. Or! So I thought.
Until my Angel said to me, don't worry,
your man has seen little his boy, cuddled him,
 wept with joy, and asked him to take care of mum,
and with the rising of the sun, the baby cried.
I saw his daddy by his side. Full of pride.so content,
as he watched our child yawn.
He waved goodbye, his duty done,
took my Angels hand, and they were gone.

Now I welcome the birth of another dawn.
Knowing he was here all along.

ONE SEED

If life blighted wanton seeds sown into fallow minds.
If for the want of watering rain falls on stony ground,
not touching open invitation.

If by sunless sky we feel the weight of clouded thought,
do we tread uncharted lanes in trepidation?
Or! Invite timeless energy into wasted space,
to fill the void. To give chase to windblown strands
of drifting thought, dissolving as a snowflake.
A melting moment that cannot stay

if only!
If only one seed planted had been sustained.
How different the Universe. How exquisite.
How bright the eternal flame.

How incredible the journey!
If that one seed had remained.

A TAINTED SOUL

OH how my tainted soul longs for solace!

Fair maiden didst thou wreck my sweeping thoughts of ecstasy?

What changes in the passion of your longing didst occur?

How shallow were thy feelings of remorse?

How innocent the face of deceit.

How well didst thou hide contempt and infidelity with a smile so sweet?

Yet! A vipers tongue didst drip with honeyed lies in disguise of pretence denied.

Dismissed as jealousy and in honesty did I believe those clear blue eyes as with a sigh you fell into my arms, chaste and innocent in your disguise?

My heart blinded by thy sweet caress did fall heavily as with regret...yet! My love torn aside I let the blade slip inside your heart. Swift and deadly no pain, in an instant your life was gone.

I had slain my love, my life!

I hang my head in shame!

Will my love forgive me? Because I know I never can.

I am a tainted soul!

A tortured man!

REFLECTION

A shame I spied that broken glass!

Shattered! Beyond repair lying forlornly in the grass!

What wonderful colours they displayed! Those prismatic glints from summer's sun!

Shining shards!

A thousand pieces instead of one.

Dismayed I realized what had become of my life, my dreams my unsung song.

Just as that glass I had started out intact, full to the brim of what might have been.

In fact! It may seem as I look upon the remains of a beautiful dream, we are no different that glass and I, both shattered remains of days gone by!

ORANGE ROBES

He lit up the sky with a smile so bright
his eyes twinkled like stars, such was his delight!
A velvet smooth voice soft as whispering winds,
soured to heavenly heights as he began to sing.

This beautiful man so modest and serene
seemed in a dream as he chanted his song.
Sat in the lotus position wrapped in deep orange robes
He chose to be humble, to follow his road.

Leaving behind all his worldly goods, and
taking his vows into the brotherhood,
making peace with his God was all that he asked.

To live in totally harmony in a world full of love
to help anyone that came in his path.
To show compassion! To care was his chosen task.

This beautiful man sat by the road, wrapped in love
and deep orange robes, seeps into my soul and
fills me with joy, my burdens felt light, my heart skipped a beat,
as I watched in wonder at pilgrims kissing his feet.

I know now with certainty that I have been blessed,
I have touched on the best, I have been honoured
to pass by this place and be looked upon with love,
by his smiling face.

This humble man in deep orange robes
just sat there serenely a smile on his face
and I knew I'd been in the presence of his Holy Grace.

EPITAPH TO A BYGONE AGE

If only life could be like the fairy tale books.
All milk and honey, love and joy,
boy meets girl - girl loves boy,
and Peter Pan beats Captain Hook.

Oh! How I loved those bygone days,
when summer meant we laughed and played.
Endless hours of fun were had,
life was good we saw no bad.

To lose a loved one wasn't known,
we were too young
we hadn't grown enough
to know what real hurt meant.
As yet our lives were innocent.

But! Came the time,
when we were made aware,
of pain and sorrow and real life fear.

What happened to those fairy tale books?
What ever became of Captain Hook?

COMPANY

He preyed upon the lonely!
He stalked them mercilessly!
He barged his way into their homes
and invited himself to tea.

His victims so glad of company,
never saw the wrong in him,
they just wanted to talk about family,
they never saw the danger within.

The police arrived at half past four,
alerted by the neighbours next door.
They said they heard an awful din
rushed round, but no one was in.

They knew the old lady didn't go far,
she was crippled and had no car.
"So you see we hope that we did right
calling you, but we had no choice
we're sure we heard her voice"

The police knocked down her door!
Saw the old lady on the floor.
She was gagged and bound, how sad!
He had taken everything she had.

This dear little lady, so gentle was she
only wanted some company. Instead
she was robbed and hit on the head,
just left there for dead. How cruel is that?

The perpetrator has yet to be found!
But! I am convinced that he will be run to ground.
And when he is? Well let's just wait and see
if there's justice he should get One to Three.

That dear old lady went home today.
Her wounds all healed, or so they say!
But what about those you cannot see?
They will live with her for eternity.

No more will she trust to open her door,
this little old lady of eighty four.
Could she be your neighbour?
Does she live next door?

LONE WOLF

A lone Wolf stands howling.
His cries echo over snow covered landscape.
His backdrop a silver moon.

SATIN THOUGHTS

Ribbons of light reflect satin thoughts!
As intertwined, longings joined forces
with long forgotten dreams.

So! It seemed that paradise existed
but only in the mind! I had to find the time
to break the pattern formed.

Be warned! When awaking past memories
make sure you're really tough.
For! Once awake you cannot put them back to sleep.

Why? Because you're just not strong enough.
And memories go deep.

HOW PERFECT

Casting shadows over limped forms,
moonbeams cascade in early dawn,
shimmering across silver skies, and
morning mist persists in wakening eyes.

Lying in a half filled dream a trickling stream
persistent in its languid flow of mellow mood,
eludes the very peace it seeks by seeping into
lucid sleep, and forming drops of imagery forces
to the surface the dawning of reality.

A leaf falls gently down to earth,
heralding the birth of wakening form,
as towards the dawn a vision born
of nature's seed delivers news of
perfect peace.

A heartfelt sigh as night retires,
and life breathed into days desires,
show nature has the balance right
How perfect! How surreal! What pure delight.

FIRE STOKED

Enigmatic smiles!
Such style! Such grace!
I looked upon his upturned face.
Saw the longing to redeem himself,
to leave this awful place.

He purged his soul, cleaned his shoes. Paid his dues.

But! What he didn't understand!
Was, to leave this land, abandon hope.
He had to re- evoke memories that held him here.

It is clear! Once fire stoked, a glimmer of hope
took precedence over longed for peace.
Once more to retreat into tired times.

I looked upon his face upturned!

It's no disgrace to have to choose!
And! As he bent to tie his shoes.
He saw with clarity, he had nothing left to lose.

BRACKISH WATERS

Brackish waters, tainted soil, no more will man toil upon this land.
For the hand of greed and disrespect has poisoned yet another mile of virgin earth.
No more seeds sown in pure delight in dirt that glows phosphorous at night.

Was it worth that condo? Does your conscience let you sleep well?
Knowing that you're "in part" responsible for this man made hell?

Does anyone understand or even comprehend these so called leaders of men?
Who gives them the right to decimate our lands?

When crops fail because of soured soil, and fish die in their thousands
from spilt chemicals and oil. Who holds up their hand and takes the blame?

I can tell you! No-one. Their excuse is lame. It's the weather I hear them say, do you know it rained all through May? The fish? That's a strange one
we have to say. Polluted waters? Goodness no, it just depends on which way the winds do blow.

Our bonuses! Why do you ask? 100K well that won't last. We have a standard to maintain, it's quite a task you understand to keep ahead of the other man.

I know when election time is here the polling booths I won't go near. Why waste my time and energy when all I see is poverty.

Until you find your inner man, and treat the land with respect. Why should I put my neck upon the line? Just carry on your doing fine.

SECRETS

Standing on the edge of time,
drinking in the heady scent of secrets
steeped in fermenting minds.

Weeping willows cascade as golden tears,
while emotions give way to unshed fears.
Fears kept locked in secret times,
bottled, mellowed as heady wine.

Ready now! As petals unfold their secrets to be told.
Standing on the brink, no time to think
ripened, rich, opening up to budding thoughts,
enriched with hazy memories they surface with the dawn,
as if awakened from eternal sleep,
as though they had just been born.

A NEW DAY

Enter now the dawn of
reasoning. Ebb away
darkened sky of doubt.

OFF THE HOOK

When I get to old to dream,
when all around me no longer seems reality.

When buzzing in my head won't go away
and thoughts refuse to stay,
will you take care of me?
Or like so many more
turn away and walk through the door.

Getting old is bad enough!
But when it comes with other "stuff",
Not knowing where you are or why,
not recognizing a loved one's face,
it's no disgrace, or so they say,
as embarrassed they turn away

So now I face the final truth!
No longer do they want me
under their roof.
So off I troop to God knows where,
they cannot bear to look!

And! As I leave, I hear them sigh,
"at last were finally off the hook".
And me?
I'm just a chapter in someone's book!

ARE WE HOME?

I lay awake!

My heart was light!

My spirit soured all through the night.

A tender touch, a heartfelt sigh,

I wonder what it is like to die.

If lightness of the heart, delights the soft eyes smiling, beguiled.

Then what if we in aged form, relinquish once more, the inner child.

What shape? If any do we take as through the door of
enlightenment we glide, in strange new garb.

How would we know the differences this journey makes!

Or is this just a memory from some long gone past left to dreams?
As at last the first new dawn warms our bones.

Are we still dreaming?

Or are we home?

THERE IS A JOY

There is a joy that diminishes all reason.
An ecstasy so vast it has no shore.
A craving that devours all decision.
A lust for nothingness, that lust for more.

There are Angels in pursuit of pain,
who take satanic pride in degradation
that will drag you down the hill and back again,
Hosanna-ing your sweet humiliation.

Just as a fire fanned by a hot dry wind,
or, like a flood sweeps away all will.
This wall of pleasure leaves no one behind,
no sign of life where all ones lives lie still.

So does the soul in anguish hate the joy
that soothes the hate that doth the soul destroy?

BETRAYED

Sweet innocence do not betray
nor take away, my childish dreams
please let them stay.

Let me play in trust not fear
to know my life is safe.
Only it's not very clear
as to why now every day
I hear the adults say,
"It's time to leave we must go away."

As we leave our little shack,
I'm told not to look back
as tanks crush our homes
and gunfire mows people down,
I frown! What have we done,
have we been bad? I ask my dad.

"No child," he pats my hand and says,
 "we don't belong, we cannot stay,
in a land that now betrays its own,
no longer can we call it home."

As we step now into no-man's land,
our people defiant stand, in unison
against this unseen hand.

So many have died for their belief,
no longer innocent, I cry in grief
for my childhood dream has gone,
was it ever there, did I ever belong?
Or was it fantasy all along?

A SOLDIER OF WAR

I am a soldier of war who stays behind enemy lines!

The reason easy ...those children could be mine.

Strapped to their tiny bodies bombs ready to detonate....In glory and in God's name? No my friends, this is fanaticism and pure hate.

A man's war no longer when infants are used as bait. See that little boy there? He's no more than eight.

"For the cause" chant the elders as they push that child forward into soldiers of the crown...then... Boom the dynamite detonates, and bodies lie broken on the ground.

A mother's cry of anguish as her child dies... and for what? Allah? No for glory and hate....but those adults fired not one shot.

Carnage! Murder!

(That child was one of their own) But such is their madness, their prejudice, their hate, that to them it's so easy to sacrifice a little boy of eight...who in their eyes now lives in the arms of their God. But in reality lies scattered on blood reddened sod.

STAY AND PLAY

I shared my dreams with all those in despair,
saw magic swirling in the air.
I found laughter just lying there, ready to giggle with those who
cared,
saw energy holding hands as one.

I looked around and saw the sun. Delighting in her warm caress I
found myself bursting with happiness.
So many dreams I shared today, I never want them to go away.

Do you think if I ask they will stay and play?

AQUARIUS DAWNS

Gentle breezes sweep away tangled cobwebs mirrored in the souls of translucent pools of liquid light. Reflections sparkle in unseen waters, so crystal clear, that only spirited souls know they are there.

Harmony plays sweet dreams, exquisitely balanced on fragile chords, so finely tuned that only angels, heralding the birth of enlightened beings, can hold their breath in timeless appreciation of endless beauty.

Relaxed attitudes sway on majestic limbs, held firm by nature's roots, enabling precious situations to be resolved in casual awareness of the need for tranquility.

Bare facts shrouded by unnecessary cloaks of doubt, no longer feel the need to withdraw into wondering, values become balanced by truth and discovery, leaving Earth's scales in total control of emotional needs.

Aquarius dawns and within its path, new roads open into understanding – learning and awareness.

And from these comes the need for truth, and the reawakening of cataleptic ideals, held rigid for so long in suspended captivity. Waiting, just waiting, for the now in which to confirm the dreams of yesterday as reality for all our tomorrows.

JUST ANOTHER STATISTIC

A flickering light!
A bygone age!

Oh! How I miss my yesterdays.

A seething mass of human flesh!
No identity!
Morons
Mindless crass!

Follow the crowd!
Do not dare to think!
Just wallow in your umpteenth drink!

Not spaced out yet?
Not, had enough?
Hey! Come on mate just take a puff.

Of course, man!
What do you take me for?
It's the real stuff alright!
The real McCoy.

Amphetamines?
Well maybe just one!
Hey, man! Chill out, three's what you need.
Come on you wimp!

Take some speed
It makes you fly!
No need for wings
Hey listen, mate an angel sings.

He lies there stoned!
No longer sane!

Who am I?
Cannot even remember his name!

At half past four, his life ebbs away!

Another statistic!

Another day!

RAINBOW BRIGHT

A rainbow in all its glory,
shimmers over new washed land,
bathing trees in iridescent colours,
how wonderful a vision, how silently I stand.

Entranced, I watch as the woodland comes to life,
Fairy magic abounds as I look around.
Enraptured by this wonderful show my face aglow
with wonderment I catch my breath, lest I break the spell
in this mystical magical fairy dell.

Raindrops resting on dappled leaves,
like crystal tears among the trees.
Catch rays of summer sun, reflecting
fairy wings transparent as the light
chases dreams, in forgotten times.
Or so it seems!

Silently I take my leave,
returning to my daily grind,
and leaving my spirit self behind
step into normality.

There! Do you see?
A reflection of the "real" me,
immortalized for all eternity.
In a rainbow bright
flooding the landscape in light.

Chasing rainbows!
Catching dreams!
It's not so crazy as if seems.

EVILS OF WAR

Weaving patterns stretch across lengthened shadows bringing forth transparencies of webbed intricacies.

Camouflaged by indiscreet layers of consciousness, murmurs become whispers, as thickened vowels sweeten the deadly deed about to begin.

Anguished souls mourn the death of innocence as the mighty sword of sin defies God's innocents laying them bare to vile incantations of evil.

Demonic substances creep and slither their way across consecrated ground soon to be scorched and blackened by screaming apparitions hardly recognisable as human forms.

Such is the power of greed.
Such is the damnation of man

NO SIN, NO HARM

My thoughts honed, as sharpened wit
depicts my state of mind.
Idiotic ideologies blunt such diabolic times
regardless of knife edged charm, and
disarm the enemy within, no sin no harm.

Myopic vision senses blind truth
allowing no seeing eyes to witness
what others fail to see,
revealing in clarity, abject poverty.

Talking times, splintered thoughts,
waging war on innocents, no thought you see,
as to where the next bomb will be,
only knowing it won't touch you or me.

Honing senses, sharpening minds,
no blunted edge to soften wounds
in these most terrible of times,
awareness comes in many forms,
have we really been so blind?

My idiotic wit is trying to depict
in poetic rhyme, the state of affairs
our world is in if only we took the time
to see the framework of blunt emotions
and dead eyes in our leaders and their kind.

It beggars belief, and an old adage comes to mind,
"There is none so blind as those that cannot see."
So they must open their hearts as well as minds,
and set each other free, to live in perfect harmony.

HAVE A NICE DAY

Creaking floorboards, flaking paint,
cracked windows, blocked drains.
Faded wallpaper, rotting wood.

Overgrown garden, broken slabs,
gate hanging off, barbeque naff.
Roof tiles missing, pond full of weeds,
Trains rushing past the wall at top speed.

"It's a bargain" the estate agent said.
"Just a few minor repairs and it's as good as new.
When was it built? 1902".

"The trains? Oh yes, it is a main line,
don't worry though, they're never on time.
Maybe the garden is overgrown,
it will be ok when the lawn is mown."

"A lick of paint and a nail or two,
and you'll soon have it looking good as new.
The windows why do you ask?
Yes they're original, but made to last."

"Plaster falling off the walls? Tiles missing,
what do you expect? I'm sure the owner won't object,
if your offer reflects those minor defects".

"Hey, why are you leaving? If this doesn't suit,
I've another to show you, but it's not quite as cute.
A two up and two down, it's a new build".

"Why, yes it's that one on the edge of the field.
That smell? It's the sewage plant over the hill.
Oh, come it isn't that bad, it's the hot weather we've had".

"Ok, there's just one more, look over there, the pubs next door.
Of course you can see they're a lively bunch,
it's dinner time so their having their lunch."

"You're what? Teetotal you say?
Blimey mate, I give up, I'm off.
Have a nice day".

SURVIVORS NEEDS

He flies! On threads of woven silk, crystal clear, warmed by the
sun. Action speaks in thickened tones, as stealthily he glides
on thermal air, content to flow in nature's course. No need to
be impatient, just allowing himself to be – for - when the time
is right he will know; and with swift and deadly accuracy,
interlaced with survivors' needs, he will swoop and in an instant -
no pain, his aim is true, his bloodstained talons claim their
prize, - and with triumphant cries of glee takes to his nest in
majesty, his prey for all to see.

DAWN

Moonbeams casting shadows
Limped eyes languish in the night air,
Purple haze swirls endlessly
Floating aimlessly without a care.

Vibrant bands of filtered light
Flicker, dance, and dream
For in the wake of morning mists
Or, so it would seem!

The land once more awakens
Its night-time duties done
And with a glance towards the dawn
Bows to the morning sun.

MY QUEEN

Were you but a smile away, I would not delay.
My quest would be to find your heart. In part
you would but look upon my face to fall beneath my spell.

Can you not tell how my longings go beyond the realms of reality?
Are you oblivious to my fantasy, or ignorant to its want?
This has to stop! My admiration, my obsession with your face.

I tell myself this cannot be! After all you can't see me.
I am but a pawn in my own game, my prize out of range.
No happy ever after in a castle for me, you see, you
are a Queen, and a Knight of the realm is not for me.

So! Back to reality. As I head towards the door
that will close you out of my life once more, I sigh goodbye.
I will not deny I hate to leave you hanging there in quiet repose,
in your regal clothes and diamond crown.

My Queen, my sovereign, my English rose
In your gilt edged frame your beauty glows.
There for all the world to see. Her Majesty,
in pride of place at the Tate Gallery.

REFLECTED TIMES

I cried a thousand tears on a lake of troubled dreams.
It seems, looking on reflected times that many others followed, or
went before, filling seas of parched memories in salted drops of
pain.

Insane! Or inane?

this moment, just gathered under shattered hope.
No dope! Just aching hearts torn apart by apathetic thought.

We ought to learn from past mistakes!
This ache, so intense, so relevant, keeps hold of broken parts.

Until! We depart this troubled life
then restored to former glory, whole and feeling fine
we step upon the stairway of learning, into the arms of the
Divine.

MY GUIDE

"Shall I walk beside you on your journey"? The old man asked.
Not to be unkind I said, "Sir I have many miles to travel." He replied,
"Child I have travelled far, my statue might look weak to the human eye,
but I promise I will not slow you down."

I looked around! No-one else it seemed had noticed this frail man.
His disposition serene, his voice mellow to the extreme.
What harm could there be in his company?

My plan! Ten miles a day if I walked fast, I hoped that he could last.
Two weeks have passed and in that time, it's me that lagged behind.
We sat beneath a sycamore tree and ate a meager lunch.
I asked this oh so quiet man, "Sir If I may be so bold,
how come you out pace me when your 86 years old?"

He smiled with such serenity, eyes bright with joy,
"My boy" He said and raised his head toward the northern sky,
"I have walked beside you all your life and will do so til you die"

At last I think I understand why only I could see this man
for he had been my spirit guide, had held my hand through
all life's adversities. He was walking me to my future,
for he knew where I should be.

No more would I question his presence,
he was my companion, my friend, my guide.

WHAT WONDERS

A Firefly!

A Foxglove!

A Fisher king!

Oh how these sights make my heart sing?

Meadow sweet!

Jasmine!

A swallow on the wing.

What wonders nature brings!

UNFETTERED ....FREE

Chains? What chains? If I remain yes!

But! What if? As with a kiss I loose the ties binding me.

What if? I take the reins and remain.

What chains?

Dare I stay? Or live to fight another day.

Hoorah!

Freedom!

Chains?

What chains?

Sorry I'm leaving...I've had my say!

DEADWOOD

A bough breaks! Deadwood!

Dried and gnarled the Oak tree relinquishes its hold.

No longer able to sustain life, its inhabitants scurry away not wanting to watch its struggle in the last throws of decay.

A creak! A groan! As roots exposed the cry of dying echoing on the wind.

A crash! Then an audible sigh as another victim of modern man dies.

A PIPERS LAMENT

A stagnant brook! Silent! Still.

Rain falling on distant hills!

Perfection! Nature balanced....all's well.

A lone Drummer in the distance spied!

A Piper lamenting those who died for King and country!

Never mind they had no will...kill or be killed ...I can hear them still!

Echoes on a windswept land ...where to a man they gave their life, leaving behind in abject misery...for they could not see the reason for this pain, the wives of Sixth Battalion lost in no-man's land.

And for what? A foot of ground, moss covered...grass now running red, as wounds bled their lives away. Dismay as futility dawns in unseeing eyes.

Only raven's cry!

For no-one is left to mourn those gone.

Piled high the corpses spread wide ...denied last rights.

For lying dead crucifix in hand the preacher already sits at God's right hand.

WAR should be banned!

Come brothers join hands!

Disband our armies...join in peace, so those lost in battle can rest in well-earned sleep.

UNBELIEVABLE

A crystal cove! A sparkling sea! Purity!
Atlantis lying on the sea bed! Fantasy!
Age old legends! History!

Nimbus and Cumulous! Reality!
Sun, rain and wind. Normality!
A starry night. Heavenly!

A child's laughter. Infectious!
A kitten's purr. Delectable!
A mother's love. Unconditional.

Peace of mind. Essential!
Realising all that we have. Unbelievable!

BABY DOLL

I saw her lying there. A broken doll.
Time had taken its toll.
She was cracked and old,
nearly bald. One eye closed.
No clothes as such, almost bare.

Her twisted frame grotesque.
One arm missing, leg broken beyond repair.

I plucked her gently from the shore,
and looked around. No one to claim this battered doll.
Not a soul in sight! So I placed her in my bag,
and walked home in delight.

You see, when I was a little girl,
I had a doll just like her.
I took her everywhere with me.
Then one day I dropped her in the sea.

I cried and cried, but no-one heard.
My baby doll was washed away.
I know it's absurd, but to this day,
that memory remains. No other doll was quite the same.

And as I washed off the mud and slime, my heart raced.
For on her back I could see the words I scratched
when I was eight.

They read, "If lost please return to this address,
23 Shore field Inverness".

Now thirty three with children of my own,
the sea has returned my baby doll home.
Washed up on the shore with all the debris.
She has been given back to me.

BIRTH OF REALITY

Paper moon, flights of fancy, trips beyond our time.
Heaven sent this message homeward, and now I know it's mine.

Leaves of knowledge form patterned thoughts, as they gently
glide to earth, and instinct warns that all's not well, as they come
before their birth.

Winged creatures fly with bated breath, as once they knew their
task. But! Since the birth of reality, they are forced to wear a
mask.

A mask of pretentious gatherings, a ploy to bait the unaware.

So, take heed all you night-time owls, reach out and touch your
fear.

For in the mist of time so heavily veiled now, remember how we
came about. Do not break this sacred vow.

For once dawn breaks on reality and there is nowhere else to
hide, what then? Where do we go? It is up to you to decide.

RETRIBUTION

As human forms amass against the gate of Hades, fear takes the shape of the cross.

Golden bows strung with silver threads take arms as trumpets blast the tune of disapproval, their notes flat as anticipation threads its beads of sweat on furrowed brows, creased in anxious wondering.

Forgotten memories suddenly flood the human brain, overtaking rational thoughts in their rush to be remembered, lest we forget the past atrocities. Deep dark caverns open wide as cracks, become ravines in tormented minds.

Speed on distant wings dear thoughts; chase the demons within, into oblivion. Fearful at its own harbinger of hell tepid waters run like icy fingers, frantic in their tears, to wash clean these troubled souls, flooding them with pure joy.

As Christians to the lions, demented powers fevered as they strive to right the wrongs feel no fear as the barricades once impenetrable fall like crumbling clay to lie beneath the feet of justice. Forever in its glory, and once again, evil is overcome.

I SPIED A MERMAID

I spied a Mermaid!
How delightful was she!
Amongst the rocks combing her hair.

I just sat there!
Mesmerised!
Enchanted, I continued to stare.

A dolphin played!
Darting in and out of the rocks
And!
While the Mermaid combed her locks
He called to her.

A magical sound reverberated all around!
Her voice, honey sweet, lifted me to my feet.
As note, upon crystal clear note, filled the air!
I soared!
My heart, felt free! No longer bound by limitations!
No longer earth bound!
No hesitation!

I swam towards that beautiful voice!
Knowing in my heart, I have a choice.

I chose that day to set aside
Self-doubt, mistrust and foolish pride,
And with such sincere honesty,
That Mermaid set me free.
Her beauty not just for me to see
Look! There she is still combing her hair!
As yet, of me, still unaware.

FREEZE FRAMED

On borders fringing fields of corn,
ripened, golden, swaying on the breeze,
I stood transfixed. As though I had been freeze framed.
Not knowing how this came to be,
only knowing I could not move, rooted as a tree.

Like a Monet, painted for all time,
preserved for centuries, I felt I had been immortalized.
Stood beside that field of ripened corn.

Hand steady," smile please," came the call.
I looked around, camera flashed, then reality.
I realised stupidly, it was only a picture
taken yesterday of me hanging in a Gallery
of modern art, my son the Artist of Photography,
but still! I played my part, for he chose me to be framed,
he said, "the perfect symmetry."

By the way! The name of this display hanging for all to see.

"MOTHER AGING AS RIPENED CORN"

Guess I must put this down to posterity. Thank you son!

OH SO SIMPLE

I looked upon your beauty,
my eyes misted; my hand
softly brushed your silken hair.

Like a fine spun cloth of pure Damask,
a perfect peach, a love so fine
heady as summer wine.

I reach across and smooth your brow,
longing to belong somehow.
Just watching as you breathe in natural sleep.

So deep my feelings, so pure and true,
so intertwined,
so spiritually in tune with you.

I realise, I understand,
and as I take your hand
to brush it with a kiss,
as I feel a longing in my heart,
to hold you close to me.
It's oh so simple in its complexity,

I know you realise it too,
we belong together for eternity,
your part of me, and I'm part of you.

THE ASSASSIN

I speak in tones of hushed deference.
I see with clarity a loyalists view.
Yet! When challenged by invitation,
to direct my revelations as to where,
if any, my visions lay. I would have to say,
"With anyone that paid me well".

You see as an assassin my loyalty lies with the highest bidder.
I need no disguise, I do not lie, my life is set, my destiny clear,
and if I live to see another year, my fortune will be assured.

No more poverty, no hungry belly to keep me awake.
But I know my fate! A tad too slow, just one mistake
that's all it takes to feel that fatal blow.

Then the curtain comes down on my final show.

READY TO BEGIN AGAIN

I seek sanctuary in the soul of compassion.
I ask forgiveness in the eyes of God.
I ask restoration of my sins,
I wish my life had never been.

My eyes blinded by reality,
my ears deaf to tuneless times,
my tongue silent in the wake of anxiety,
desperation inviting crime.

Feelings matter little in this sordid life I live,
no one to wonder who I am, no one to forgive.

Just another statistic, one more on the list
of wasted dreams, a blackened metaphor
of dripping veins, I ask myself, am I insane?

In an insane world where life is cheap,
where to keep body and soul together
you sell yourself for the price of a drink,
take heed, stop and think.

Claim retribution for your sins,
throw those needles in the bin,
take hold of life for all your worth,
purity began at birth.

Sullied though you might have been,
it's time now to come clean,
cleanse the body, heal the mind,
everything else will come in time.

At last! After months of detox, rehab,
mind and body cleansed,
you're ready to start living,
ready to begin again.

PERFECTLY FORMED

I watched!

Enchanted!

My heart missed a beat!

For!

Among the foliage

Perfectly formed, symmetrically spun

The purest web of gossamer silk hung

Suspended!

It seemed in thin air

Until!

I spied its creator resting,

Basking in the morning sun,

Oblivious to my admiration

Satisfied, knowing his days work was done.

RAINBOW WINGS

I came across a fairy ring one day,
Long ago, in early spring.
Plaintive cries of birds in song,
Drew me to a woodland brook
And there just as in the books,
A fairy sat brushing golden locks,
Gossamer wings fluttered as she sang.
Her voice honey sweet, her laughter,
tinkling on the breeze.
She looked my way, smiled,
Held out her hand "Come – come with me.
Welcome to our fairy realm my friend..
You are blessed with vision
Clear and true.
I have been waiting a long time for you."

I followed her with bated breath
Soon, a wonderland came into view.
A myriad of colours dazzled my eyes,
Rainbow wings of every size
Hovered near, as excited voices caught my ear,
"She has come! She has come!"
Now all will know we are not a myth
A longing, a sigh of "What if?"

How long I stayed, I cannot say
But to this very day,
I remember every second spent in that woodland glen
I was in my element.

What have I done with those memories?
I've written them down for all to read.
So take your time, peruse my words,
You know what to do when you hear the birds.

NO ONE AT HOME!

I fly alone!
As usual!

No one at home!
Surprise!

No longer do I bemoan my fate
I left!
Injured!
Wounded heart!

But!
Did we part?
Who knows!

When longings die, and shadows
Cast their cloak of doubt.
Why stay!
What is the delay?

Redemption sits as ghostly judge
As souring into heights unknown.
I become myself.
Whole again.
But so bereft!
And so alone!

No one at home!

A LONELY GULL

A lonely gull cried piteously
his screech echoed on the wind
as if he sensed the danger he was in.

A frozen landscape trapped in
winters sleep, lies wrapped in a snow
covered blanket three foot deep.

A watery morning sun tries it's
best to warm the land, and failing
in its task bows down to natures hand.
Silence creeps as slippered feet,
across these barren lands,
and thickened tones of innocence
try to understand.

Fingers of tapered longings
stroke life into the very core
of passive undercurrents,
as waves of emotion lap the shore.

Frozen peaks of passion at last begin to thaw,
and nature renews its energy,
who could ask for more?

THE BIRTH OF REALITY

Undamaged tireless harbingers of fate, Immaculate Conception bids Our Lady wait. Investitures of lightened souls pour forth our unborn dreams, and charity bestows its gift of platitudes it seems.

Innocuous substances fall right before our feet, in oh such feeble attitudes of chances that we would meet. Destiny now plays a hand in seraphicial style, and bids us wait, to bide our time just for a little while.

In all its trident glory, within its natural glow, a burst of iridescent light shines bright in liquid flow. A mass of molten ashes smouldering hot and coldly white take over every fibre of human emotions late at night.

"Hark!" listen to the fables; understand the need to know just how the world renewed its faith in one glorifying show.

A thousand voices chanted, leaving man without a doubt, that only pure prayer and positivity could save our planet so.

And as we grow within the realms of light and understanding, as the veils of wistful yesterdays, leave humanity trembling. One wonders as the candles glow in meditative state, how can we rectify our wrongs? How can we change our fate?

A BUTTERFLY

I am as delicate as a butterfly, alone and feeling sad.
I tried to analyse this strange dream I had.
I remembered feeling lost and faltering as I flew.
I landed on a lily pad full of morning dew.

My wings became useless as I tried to fan them dry.
My heart was pumping furiously as I found I couldn't fly.
My senses alert in case danger lurked nearby.

I lay so very still! I knew that I could die
then a gentle hand plucked me from that lily pad,
and an Angel I did spy. I cannot deny how safe I felt
in that loving space. My Angel stroked my face!

Now I understand my dream!
It would seem I had no place to go.
I had been feeling low, and so alone
I had flitted like a butterfly, with no place to call "home"

I had tried to find my way that day and felt that I would drown.
What I should have realised is, my Angel would never let me down.

A TANNER A GO

A tanner a go!
Don't be slow!
Show the missis
the strength in yer arm.

Cor blimey mate!
You've ad one over the eight
best put er down,
before she comes to some harm.

A tanner a go!

Alright young man,
throw as hard as you can,
no! Not at yer old man,
at the row of tin cans,
oh blow!
Yer knocked off the lot
all in one throw.

A tanner a go!

Come on young lady,
don't you be shy
give it a go
ouch!
Right in my eye.

A tanner a go!

Do yer know!
I think I'm off home.

My eye is a sight,
the wife will swear I've
been in a fight,

that's me locked
out for the night.

A tanner a go!

A MIRACLE

I walk in the garden of enlightenment.
I tread the path of dreams.
I seek solace in solitude.
Life is not what it seems!

As I swing on a moonbeam.
As I follow a star.
As I bask in the sun's golden rays.
I swim with the tide. Oh! Happy days.

Enlightenment comes with understanding.
Dreams show me the way.
Solitude brings contentment.
In this life I would like to stay.

So I will go with the tide.
Shine bright like a star,
spread sunshine wherever I go,
and in doing so, hope like the moon I will glow.

One of life's little miracles happened today!
It's bought joy to my heart, light in my dark,
my faith is restored, my eyes see anew.

That miracle? Lord, I believe in you!!

THE PREY

He stalked the deer relentlessly

Bow and arrow at the ready

She weaved her way through tangled briar, bracken tearing loose,

And suddenly within her sight

A huge majestic Moose.

Stamping ground! Snorting! Head lowered in preparation,

The young deer standing, shaken, panting hard in trepidation.

He swings the bow, arrow pointing, lining up its foe.

Then, without warning, his arrow left the bow!

The deer took off in panic!

Veering right! Escaping!

The arrow was too slow!

Instead of him reloading, his prey now lost, long gone

The Hunter realised, just too late

The Moose, his anger roused, was bearing down upon his foe.

The tables had been turned, the fear that poor deer felt was metered out to the Hunter now the hunted, do you think he felt that killer blow?

ECHOES ON THE WINGS OF TIME

I awoke! And Spring was on my heels
Foxglove, Primrose, Daffodils.
Their perfume haunting, memories awoke
Of childhood dreams and fairy folk.

"Not again!" My mum would say,
As I skipped and danced along the way
Towards my favourite woodland path,
"Leave her luv, she's not daft.
Just wistful, imaginative, a child's fantasy,
You know, don't know what she expects to see!"

Aye! Fairies, goblins, elves and gnomes,
Fairy rings and magic stones
that glisten in the morning sun.
"She is strange that lass, best left alone,
She will no doubt understand one day,
And all her dreams will fade away."

Echo's on the wings of time
Voices long gone. Like summer wine.
I matured with age
But! I never did turn the page.

Still and silent I listen now
"Do you hear them too? I do avow.
Those woodland folk are fit and well,
Was that larkspur, bird's eye and bluebells?
Twinkling in the evening sun.

Why there's a fairy dancing on every one.
So why not keep those childhood dreams.
Or are they real? Ask yourself
'Cause nothings really as it seems.'

HOLD THE MEMORY

Morning awakening mankind!

Lengthening shadows hold the light,

As infinite wisdom so often lost in thought,

Emerges as a lightened beam of understanding.

Once more to hold the memory, so easily lost,

As consciousness comes to the fore,

Shutting out dreams of nights repose.

Reluctantly we rise!

And finally, let go.

JUSTICE

I feel the blood pulse through my veins!
His eyes glint menacingly he looks insane!
He sneers!
He laughs! Demonic!
Terrible noises growl from his throat,
 as he lashes out and breaks my nose.

I cover my face with blood red hands!
He sneers again! Enjoying my pain!
So you think you can escape my blows!
Ha! He cries and again pummels my nose.

My eyes by now swelling fast!
He punches me, as he saunters past.
I'm off to the pub you slovenly b----ch,
give me some money,
I only married you because you're filthy rich.

I walked calmly to the drawer! He looked!
He couldn't be sure of what I would pull out
from that inner place.
A glance in the mirror showed my face!

And! As my hand touched the gun
I knew with a smile I had won.
No more would he meter out pain!
No more, his evil laugh
as I took the blame for his drunken rage!

The bullet found its mark!
His mocking done!
I calmly put down the gun!

And!
As I walk free from court today
I can honestly say!
I'd do it again!

As I turn the last page!
And I close the book
on my battered life
I take a last look!
I realise I'm free, I'm off the hook!

MUSIC

Into delights of feathered dreams and long gone memories resurrected it would seem in nights repose, eyes flickering as the scene unfolds, came symphonies, not yet born still in embryotic state.

A cacophony of stringed quartet, a Harpist, Cello, Percussion all mingled in my cataleptic sleep. So deeply did I feel the pain of exquisite tune that as yet had no name?

So sweetly did those notes unfold, so beautifully honed, as if I'd known that every cipher jotted down would somehow match the ones before? A fire, desire to compose a masterpiece, yet roused from sleep I had no knowledge of music, only that to hear a piece of Mendelssohn or Strauss, Tchaikovsky, Brahms, to fall into the arms of every note would choke emotions, leave me spent, my love of music evident.

As once again the music flows I slumber in my night's repose, I'm drawn into a chamber deep within my mind. How could I have been so blind?

Only in this lifetime have I turned away from composing, I have to say, eyes wide open I see who I was, where I belonged. My name is of no consequence .... I am now long gone.

PILLS

"Take two a day", I heard the Doctor say.
"Not with the four you already take,
make sure you have an hours break".

"Ok", I said! "But what about the pills
you gave me for my head?
"Do I take those as well?"
"Of course!" he said.
"Just take three before you go to bed".

I walked out of the surgery, confused!
Now which one do I take with food?
Is the red one for my head?
Or do I take the blue instead?

Do you know I am feeling ill?
Bewildered by these bl-----dy pills,
I think they're going down the drain
I won't be going to the doc's again!

AN OPEN GATE

I listen, I see, I think and I feel!
I laugh and I cry, go low and go high.
I ask myself, is this life for real?

I often feel its passing me by
and nobody cares how hard I try
to fit into societies social "bit".

I wonder just how long it will take!
Until I'm allowed through an open gate.
No more "you don't belong,
or paying the piper for somebody's song.

I know one day soon the light will shine through
when man takes a stand united and true.
No more them and us, but you and me,
holding hands singing "Land of the free".

PERFECT BALANCE

The World spins!

An Angel sings!

Perfect balance in all things!

NEARLY DONE

Toxic waste! Big disgrace!
Vile fumes! Cities doomed!

Well! That's what the papers say.
I read it only yesterday!

Mayan calendar now done.
If we listen to the doom and gloom,
we're all waiting for the big boom,
it's meant to happen December 21.

So! How come the centre page
is advertising the latest rage? For Christmas that is!

My question is this!

"If we're all going up with a bang,
there will be no stocking to hang.
So why are we being pushed to buy
all this stuff if we're going to die"?

I think that the answer to all of this,
is the media are taking the p----s.
It seems they will print anything today.
As long as they get their take home pay.

My advice to all would be to say!
"Fold up the paper, and put it away.
Just enjoy Xmas don't look at the news,
after all we don't want the New Year blues."

GRIEF

Flooded landscapes match my tears.

Howling winds define my screaming mind.

Leafless trees bare my heart.

REALMS OF FANTASY

In the realms of fantasy, take note of all you see.
For when reality claims rationality, and silences the mind,
Beware your secret longings do not get left behind.

Freedom holds with bated breath memories of time.
Sweet parodies of enchantment breathe life into the sublime.
Intoxicating self-made dreams as heady as summer wine.

Steered gently by serenity, coaxed with loving kind,
Shadows of harboured longings, once hidden ne'er to shine,
Burst forth in unchained harmony, and touch upon the divine.

Melting moments! Liquid times flow gradually on course,
Melding into happiness as they finally reach the source.

TOMORROWS DAWN

The past lies buried deep.

Today's shadows shape tomorrow's dawn.

The future becomes yesterday's courage

HOW ENCHANTING

Iridescent colours! Circles within circles! Fragility of mind! Life in its simplicity! Time sublime. Stolen kisses! Wisps of cotton candy! Childlike enthusiasm! How innocent! How divine!

Catching moonbeams! Touching stars! Travelling on clouds of dreams, how carefree is my heart.

Bathing in its warming glow sunshine puts on a show relaxed and feeling fine. Circles within circles, everlasting! How enchanting! How wonderfully divine.

DEEP BROWN EYES

Evocative, provocative, tantalizing, pure.
Emotive, sublime, delightfully demure.
Radiant, dazzling, electrifyingly alive.
Iridescent, sparkling as pools of liquid light.

Sinking into depths unknown, drowning with desire.
I gaze into your deep brown eyes, flashing as on fire,
and realize I am hopelessly lost. No way can I survive,
without your look of tenderness to keep my heart alive.

RESCUED

He wore a fisherman's hat!
I stood alone on the shore!
No more!
The words had slipped quietly from my tongue,
then I realised, I was not alone!

"What ails you my child?" Asked the man.
"Tell me, I will help you if I can."
"Sir!
I've no one I can trust,
so many times I've loved and lost,
my heart can take no more,
that's why you see me by the shore."

He came and stood by my side,
and said "Child where's your pride?
Do you not realise your worth?
Why do you think you're here on Earth?"

"Your birth was planned,
Make no mistake,
your life is not yours to take.
You will not be alone for long,
to you a son will soon be born!

I turned to say, "I understand."
no longer would I mourn the man,
I'd lost at sea months before,
no longer walk along that shore
with suicide in mind.
How could I be so blind?

But when I turned to thank the man
there was only one set of footprints in the sand!

FOR THE LOVE OF HER PACK

With stealth she crawled through the undergrowth, her ears and eyes alert. She skirted past several of her kind snuggled upon the earth.

The time was now to make her stand, she held fast her growing fear, for, she knew without a doubt her enemy was near.

It's said that courage comes in many forms, that day was no exception. She felt her muscles tense, her body shimmered on the lake mirroring her reflection.

When later on they found her form, still and sleek and dead, the humans knew on a fool's errand there'd been led. The sacrifice she made that day by leading then astray showed she had no need to defend her pack she for had led the hunters away.

The legend goes that on a summer's night her form walks silhouetted against the moon, she howls in promise of the dawn and carries new life in her womb.

A NEW MOON

Into the wilderness stepped my heart, longings scattered on barren ground. No sound! Silence! Audible! Questing! Vibrating!

Hesitating, the pulse of life stilled, chilled, yet white hot heat pumped a rhythm, a beat as tapping feet.

Barely heard, finely tuned, so delicate, so surreal to heal the wounds of blighted soil. To foil landscape naked in its rustic tones.

Honed to synchronize animated form Dawn challenges Night. No fright just flight.

Hostility tamed! A new frame! A picture completed, nature reborn. Heart restored, balance retained ready to beat in perfect tune

A new moon.

MINDFUL LONGINGS

Are we not caught by ridged thoughts and tantalised by swaying fronds of hapless dreams, into summoning our inner self to redeem that which so long has captured minds in unsung song?

Are we therefore mindful of longings not yet formed, waiting in anticipation in foetal pose, to strike the heart of love in sweet repose?

Do we dare to chance in destiny, or should evoked emotions wait no more as summoning inner strength we step with perfect peace through an open door?

What more could one ask? To lay bare emotions in flickering dreams, reality it seems stands back allowing holiness of innocence, in reverence to that most sacred of place, that inner space.

Love for humanity shared with grace.

HEARTACHE GONE

In the longings of my heart I feel the stirrings of life. A flutter, a feather like touch, just enough to show that light shines on a darkened hue of doubt.

Visions cloaked in Purple mists once obscured, resist the urge to fall into space having found their place.

And now! Renewed, energised into clarity, no charity, for alert, awakened by the kiss of love, power seeps in through every vein. Not just blood, but a blending of two vital forces of life. Flowing freely now that doubt has gone. Replaced not by fear of unsung song, but awakened dreams. Dreams that had hovered near the surface for so long, now to be revealed.... Heartache gone.

WOODSTOCK

In Woodstock dare I tread the boards of delighted gift? Or! Intentions pure (though I have to admit) to touching on moods of discontent, where, unless advertised as secured moments, timed precisely right, I am want to stumble unprepared into darkened night.

In flight, momentarily stilled as wingless breath holding on to hopeless thought (less the spell of mediocrity takes precedence over innocence) I speak in hushed tone.

Alone! And in those stippled times finding reverence in coloured thought I am myself! Ready now those boards to walk.

SNAPSHOT

It seems all summer long, when darkest days have disappeared, that even in the midst of balmy breath you freeze.

Not as with cold nor fear. But! It would seem this time of year camera at the ready, lest the moment be lost, you halt, mindful that to lose the now....unless captured in positive frame, you could not look back in clarity as nothing would remain the same.

Smile...so the moment is retained.

THE BRIDE

In summers misty morn fair maiden rise. For in the flush of dawn, eyes open as you look upon thy lovers face mirrored in reflected gaze, take note of form, of sleeping breath of whispered words and silent caress.

Gently does your heart beat as one as melded into lifelong dreams it would seem your journey of togetherness has just begun.

MY EPITAPH

I stared at the lectern, but! I didn't know why.
Never before had it taken my eye!
I stared at the book!
Lying dusty and worn.
A page half open, all tatty and torn.

My heart beat so fast!
I thought I would die,
instead I just crumbled,
and started to cry.

For there, on that page,
words started to form,
and suddenly!......Suddenly!

The truth slowly dawned.,
The tears being shed
were for me, I am dead!, I'm being mourned!

As they carry my coffin out
down the path.
I realised!

I had read my own epitaph!

COMPASSION

Brave heart dost thou not taste the joys of victory yet turn thy head away in defeat?

Why when the battles nearly won and glory shines upon you as the sun do you decide to turn and run?

To shun the might of majesty, to defy the heroic act, that in fact would give to you the precious gift of mighty warrior.

Epic tales would down the centuries tell of your might. What right do you have to wage a war of discontent?

It was not meant to be this way, you were supposed to slay thine enemy. Yet instead that act of so called "cowardliness" has left you dead.

Compassion was thy crime...alas sadness now is mine.

TENDER TIMES

In tender times waste not the thought of youth...but rather look into the eyes of masked reality. Turn the tides of sweeping dreams, and in rationality heed the contemptuous lust of enemies, and face hard truth.

As once in youth we did succumb to temptation, only to be told the truth...that age defies rationality and guides the guiless through shattered times. Until stilled! The mind begets original thought, that ought we not to live in exulted times?

No crime! No avarice! Sublime though noxious thought takes all we deemed as just, and turns matter into matter then dissolves it all to dust.

PERFECTION

In the embryonic state of dreams it seems no longer do we fear our fate. For! When we wake from sweet repose a child-like vision a rosy glow of nurtured thoughts show us where we ought to be.

You see we are perfection! Here for all our eternities, it's time to start the show.

THE DAY MY LIFE CHANGED

I vowed not to cry, sniffed, and wiped a tear from my eye. My gaze fixed on a cloudless blue sky. I asked myself why? Why can you not break down and cry? The answer was clear...now would mum really approve? Could you imagine her glare? So I just stand here and stare.

Singing (I can hear it in the distance somewhere) prayers filter over my head, I really don't care.

It's a strange kind of day! People milling around, sympathies muttered, sobbing abounds. "Get lost in your dreams" mother would say, "Just pretend it's not happened and it will go away"

If only! If only those words could come true. This days changed my life.....strange the sky is still blue. The sun is still shining, hurting my eyes. No I'm not crying as I say my goodbyes. The sun is so strong, that's why I sigh.

This days changed my life....but I cannot think why!

TROUBLED THOUGHTS

In absent minds abstracts appear as splintered light igniting fear of unknown foe.

Shall we stand and fight, or just let go?

Shadows flicker!

Mind alert!

No!

Just a glimpse of other worlds, shaking shattered ideals in silent recognition of the self.

Fractured sentences break down incessant dreams accumulated in harboured sleep, extracting incomprehensible words from garbled tongue, as bit between the teeth slacks, and emotions tumble out.

How strange the human mind. How weak!

Examine now your Universe!

Still that broken soul!

For as we speak, or think! So does the memory awake within the glow of day?

Take solace from an untrained eye ... blink...it might just go away!

A MUG OF TEA PLEASE

Each day he sits there all alone, a blanket wrapped around his form.

This ragged man asked little from me as I passed him by, "Just a mug of tea please." I hear him cry.

So on to the bakery for a breakfast roll and tea," Two spoons of sugar a dash of milk please." "Thanks Luv that will be two pound three."

Hugging my scarf tighter, gloved hands toasty and warm, I head towards that ragged man...oh he looks so forlorn!

"Here my friend have breakfast on me, no need for thanks it's just a cup of tea. The rolls still hot so eat it please, and while I think of it here take these from me."

His hands were blue, his blanket thin so I gave my scarf and gloves to him!

"You're a fool!" someone said as they sauntered by with bent head, "The town looks bad enough as it is, without his kind to make it worse...watch out he doesn't steal your purse."

I learnt a good lesson on that day, that man had nothing yet I heard him pray, "Thank you Lord for the food I eat, kindly watch over the woman who didn't pass me by, who didn't leave me here to die."

How much did it cost to help that man?

Do you think you might try to feel the plight, of homeless people alone and hungry day and night?

I know we can make a difference if we try...no one should be left out in the cold to die.

Two pounds for a roll and a cup of tea...really how difficult can that be?

Sleep well in your cosy bed tonight knowing you have helped someone in need...it's a warm toasty feeling so thank you from me!

A PALE PINK MOON

A pale pink moon shining low and bright...rainbows of colour lending their light. Inviting ghosts of journeys untold into Galaxy's unknown, yet to behold!

FAITH

Tempered steel sliced through severed thoughts.
Fragmented ideas structured isolated misdeeds,
and energy slowly, so as not to break the cord of discontent,
awoke in fear and trepidation, ready for the curse of day.

As molten lava, vile words spilled hot and deadly,
open cuts, bloody, spewed from mangled flesh,
as hate and cruelty took their toll,
and thousands lay there dead.

God in all his wisdom, looked down taking stock,
unable to comprehend what's happening to his flock.
An Angel stood by his side, and cried,
"How many chances can you give them Lord?"
He smiled, his eyes tinged with sorrow, and said,
"Until they learn the truth, or all are dead.".

"We have to trust in those who know
the reason for their birth, the seekers of the truth,
who now walk upon the Earth".

"Do not fear for them my trusted friend,
for as you know, they are locked in mortal combat,
though not as one would suppose,
look there on that bloody battlefield,
see! Among the dead and dying a beautiful red rose".

A host of golden angels plucked those souls one by one,
until, by the setting sun, not one remained,
no dead, no dying, no maimed,
for in his ultimate love for all,
he had picked those fallen flowers,
and in his garden they will stay.

So at night, when we pray for peace on Earth,
remember what the good Lord said,
he has faith in us to do what's right,
so the World can sleep without fear at night.
Remember! We are all children of the light.

YOUR GUIDE

I walk beside you every day,
hold your hand along the way,
smooth your brow as you sleep
and promise you your soul to keep.

I lift you when you're feeling down,
make you smile instead of frown,
and catch your tears before you drown.

I will be with you along your path
I will cherish you in life and death,
I will wrap you in a cloak of love
but most of all I promise you this,
I will never ever leave your side.

I am your Guardian Angel, your protector your guide.

Printed in the United States
By Bookmasters